Make
a Rocket

by Jackie Walter and Lucy Makuc

Make a rocket

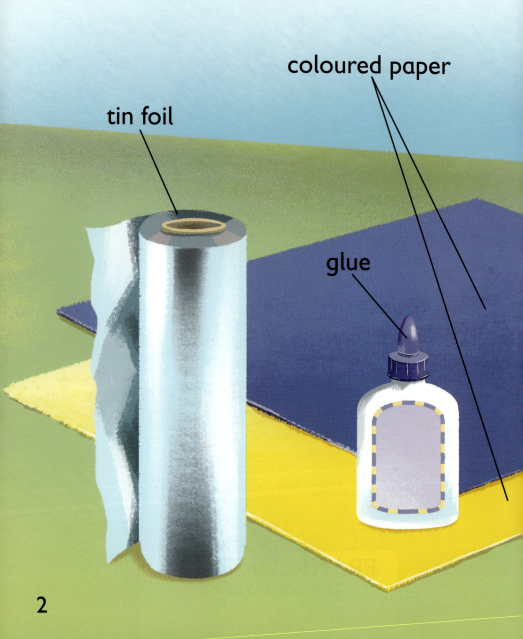

coloured paper

tin foil

glue

plastic bottle

scissors

sticky tape

Get some paper.

Cover the bottle with
the paper.

Tape the paper to the bottle.

Get some more paper.

Make a cone.

11

Tape the cone on top
of the rocket.

Cut some foil.

Cut out some shapes.

Here is the rocket.

Talk and Explore

Ask your child to describe each picture below, in their own words, pointing to each picture in turn.

Look together at the objects needed to make the rocket and then how each item is used.

Independent Reading

This series is designed to provide an opportunity for your child to read on their own. These notes are written for you to help your child choose a book and to read it independently.

In school, your child's teacher will often be using reading books which have been banded to support the process of learning to read.

Use the book band colour your child is reading in school to help you make a good choice. *Make a Rocket* is a good choice for children reading at Yellow Band in their classroom to read independently.

The aim of independent reading is to read this book with ease, so that your child enjoys the story and relates it to their own experiences.

About the book
Follow this instructional text on how to make a homemade rocket using everyday materials.

Before reading
Help your child to learn how to make good choices by asking: "Why did you choose this book? Why do you think you will enjoy it?" Look at the cover together and ask: "What do you think the book will be about?" Support your child to think of what they already know about the topic. Read the title aloud and ask: "What things do you think will be used to make the rocket? Why do you think that?" Remind your child that they can try to sound out the letters to make a word if they get stuck.

Decide together whether your child will read the story independently or read it aloud to you. When books are short, as at Yellow Band, your child may wish to do both!

During reading

If reading aloud, support your child if they hesitate or ask for help by telling the word. Remind your child of what they know and what they can do independently.

If reading to themselves, remind your child that they can come and ask for your help if stuck.

After reading

Support understanding of the book by asking your child to tell you what they found out. Did they learn anything new? Did anything surprise them?

As you discuss the book, you might begin to use vocabulary such cut, stick, paste, measure, draw, and wrap.

Give your child a chance to respond to the book: "Can you think of other things that you could add to the rocket?"

Use the Talk and Explore activity to encourage your child to talk about what they have learned.

Extending learning

Talk about the materials used in the book, and where you can find them. Discuss the importance of following each step of the instructions in order and not missing any steps out.

Think about what other objects you could make with these materials and write some step-by-step intructions for them.

In the classroom, your child's teacher may be introducing punctuation.On a few of the pages, check your child can recognise capital letters and full stops by asking them to point these out.

Franklin Watts
First published in Great Britain in 2021
by The Watts Publishing Group

Copyright © The Watts Publishing Group 2021

Series Editors: Jackie Hamley and Melanie Palmer
Development Editors and Series Advisors: Dr Sue Bodman and Glen Franklin
Series Designers: Cathryn Gilbert and Peter Scoulding

A CIP catalogue record for this book is
available from the British Library.

ISBN 978 1 4451 7505 8 (hbk)
ISBN 978 1 4451 7580 5 (pbk)
ISBN 978 1 4451 7506 5 (library ebook)
ISBN 978 1 4451 8342 8 (ebook)

Printed in China

Franklin Watts
An imprint of
Hachette Children's Group
Part of The Watts Publishing Group
Carmelite House
50 Victoria Embankment
London EC4Y 0DZ

An Hachette UK Company
www.hachette.co.uk

www.franklinwatts.co.uk

FSC
www.fsc.org
MIX
Paper from
responsible sources
FSC® C104740